Life Needs Salt...
and maybe a little sugar

Jullea Powell

BookLeaf Publishing

Life Needs Salt... and maybe a little sugar ©
2023 Jullea Powell

Presentation by *BookLeaf Publishing*

Web: www.bookleafpub.com

E-mail: info@bookleafpub.com

ISBN: 9789357441667

First edition 2023

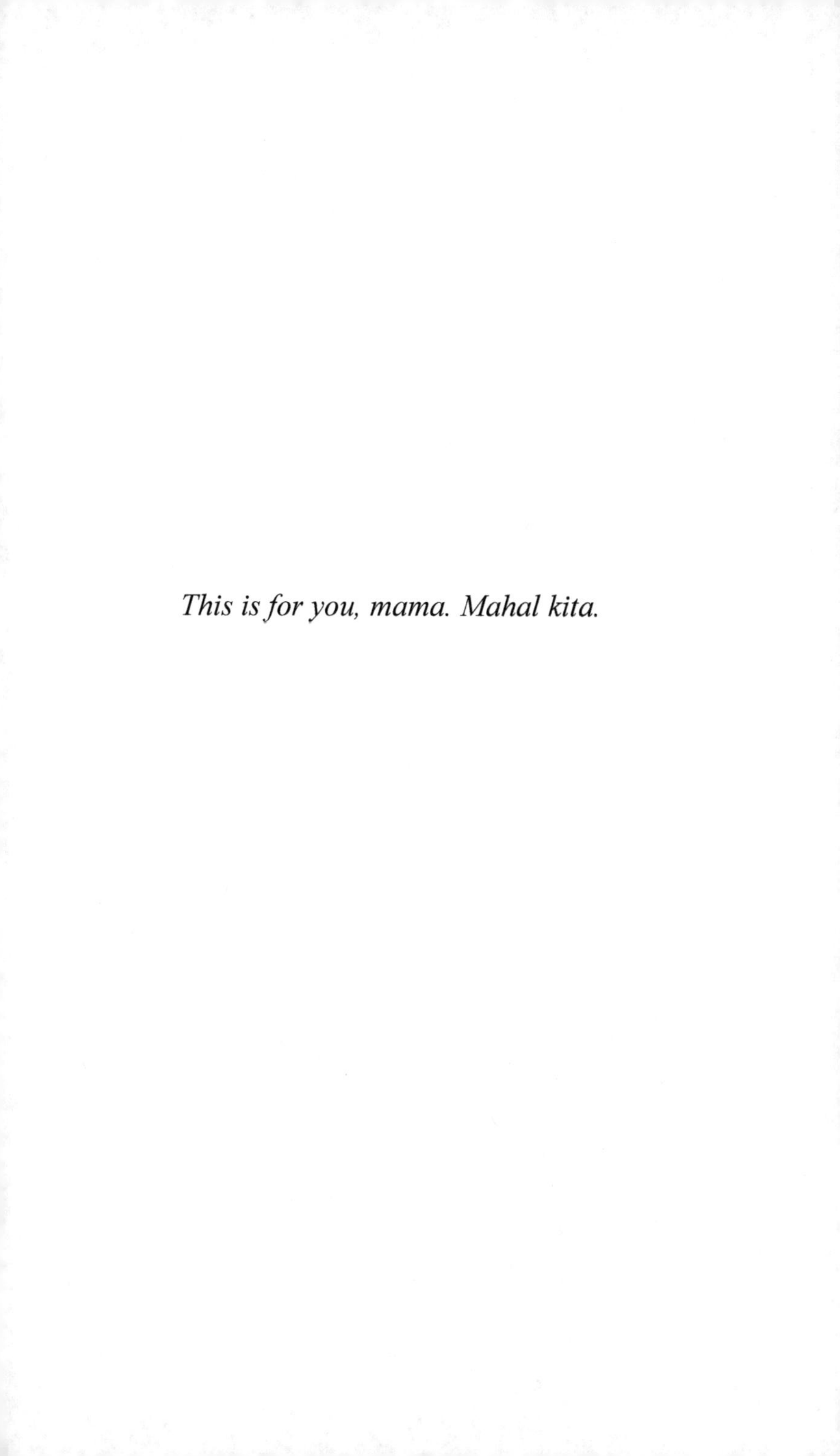

This is for you, mama. Mahal kita.

ACKNOWLEDGEMENT

Verbally sparring with dad & teaming up with mom gave my writing some charm.

PREFACE

Poetry is writing with loose, open ends, which is the reality of life; unpredictable, with much unfinished and left for interpretation. Whether tangible or intangible, our memories and collectibles are poems unsaid, which is what this poetry book is comprised of. Perhaps all our stories are variations of the same poems.

Drive Into New Year Fireworks

Cruising down the interstate,
The city lights of San Francisco fading.
Planes becoming shooting stars,
The brightest one destined for the Philippines.

One hand on the wheel,
One hand clasped with mom,
One tick striking midnight,
Dozens of fireworks sprinkling the black sky.

Blurry flares of color
Exploding through central and peripheral views,
Seen through the crying windshield,
As wipers wash away the tears.

Sparking fireworks replacing city lights,
Singing drowning out pops and raindrops,
Syncing into a singular melody,
Driving into the new year.

Twenty-Letter Love Medications

Hospitals confuse the average person.
Liquids ranging the color spectrum,
Labyrinths of tubes weaving in and out of
patients,
But everyone has the same broken heart
When a loved one is diagnosed with cancer.

Hearing the medications mom is on,
With 20 letter names and impossible
pronunciations,
I don't know what scares me more;
My ignorance of medical jargon,
Or deciphering their meanings.

While everyone expects the bald head,
Most don't notice the loneliness
Through the piles of flowers and cards.
For hours of chemotherapy and transplantation
20 letter medications are the only constant in
cancer.

Resentful Appreciation

Using appreciation to suppress resentment,
Is a dangerous experiment.
For while you're weighing the appreciation,
The resentment scale will break.

The resentment scale exceeded maximum
capacity,
Because no one paid attention to the rising
levels.
And while compensating with the appreciation
scale,
It did not as much twitch.

But how can we zero out the resentment scale?
For this neglected scale does not spontaneously
combust.
While regular maintenance is necessary,
The first step is recognizing the weight gain.

Solace in the Sand

Sparkling scarlet sand,
Glittering drops flowing to land,
Each drop descending 15 feet,
The pristine white cascade squeezed,
Beneath the narrow concave canyon walls;

The wet metal ladder
Holding steadfast to the falls;
Despite being completely drenched
Ascending this slippery ladder,
I was as carefree as drops surrendering to
gravity.

Shimmering sunkissed tanned skin,
Matching perfectly with pastel rocks
And the rainbow above the falls.
As a social butterfly alone in the desert,
Solitary serenity had never provided so much
solace.

Baklava Hurrah

5

Flaky filo layers
Fluttering in the oven
Baked to golden brown
With translucent honey drops
Sprinkling sparkles of pistachio atop
Juicy pistachio filling oozing out the sides
Baklava's flavor exploding like lava
I guess I left a piece of my heart in Turkey,
A land I've never been.

Flying Hellos & Goodbyes

Looking at the airport screens,
Seeing dozens of times and places,
Thousands of people moseying around,
With accents from all corners of the world,
Styling Chanel bags and hoodie bed heads.

And amidst anticipating my adventure,
I see people with signs and flowers,
Squashed between an airtight hug.
Hopefully someday I'll know a bit of the whole
wide world,
With teary eyed hellos & goodbyes at every
airport I go.

Music To Infinity

Music is the ticket to infinity and beyond,
Free of charge with no one able to barge.
A world full of dreams & tears breaking the
soul's seams
A way to reach to dream destinations
Or return to the homeland the heart bittersweetly
yearns.

Reliving our lives or imagining others,
Remember lost loved ones,
To feel empowered at life changing events,
Or simply vulnerable in solace,
Music romanticizes every moment to power
through.

Free as a Ski

8

A drop of snow on my nose,
A tangible reminder that ski season is amidst.
While bumping and swinging on the chairlift,
Going up into the cloud of refreshing mist,
Free as a ski as gravity tugs me down the slope.

As skis crunch the powdered snow,
Forming crisply cursive swirls of tracks,
Powdered slopes are washed away like soap.
Feeling like a cup of cocoa in my winter coat,
With a breeze from speed on the slopes.

Love Letters Deserve Love

Oh, to receive a love letter.
Whether romantic or platonic,
Someone expressing their feelings,
And fondest memories of us,
Just seems like quite a dream.

Though I'd never complain
About receiving a crisp 50 dollar bill
In a mass-produced Hallmark card,
After all it is the thought that counts;
If only thoughts were more personal.

1st (of November) Place

Being a November 1st birthday,
Most people my special day as:
The day after Halloween,
All Saints Day,
Even World Vegan Day.

As I blew out my 17 candles,
I wished with my cross
And all my good luck charms
That I'm destined for my dream college.
Being a junior in high school,

I knew that exactly one year
From when the clock struck midnight,
The application for my dream college is due.
Hopefully my hard work and birthday wish,
Will suffice an acceptance.

Heart of Jewels

I don't quite have a heart of gold,
Though I'd say it's comprised of jewels.
Shifting colors in the sun and gloom,
Smooth and fragile,
But a bit raw and rough.
Despite my frazzled brain,
Frizzy hair,
Crinkled Sweats,
And tired eyes,
At least the ring on my finger
And my heart of jewels
Still shine.

Quirks of a Chirp

No one forgets their first pet,
Or more so their first bird.
The rainbow feathers of my first sun conure,
Brighter than my brown orbs of ecstacy.

For when your bird is on your steering wheel,
Trying to snag a bite of toast;
You feel him land on your shoulder with a
swoosh,
And you only want to give him a smooch.

Whether it be a chirp of excitement
Or squawk of hunger,
You can't help but have a soft spot,
Even as he tears keys off your keyboard.

As the bird develops his favorite songs,
Bobbing his head to the beat,
Cocking his head in confusion as to why you
shut it off
You bittersweetly weep, remembering Cobble
Pot is gone.

Sleepless Nights &
Bittersweet Smiles

What is the balance
Between sleepless nights
With dreams in mind
And family reunions
And all-nighters with friends?

My family is proud
Of my straight As and accolades
And I am too
Knowing my sleepless nights
Became a trophy that's quite a sight.

At my busiest I've disappointed friends
Who never seem to care about my dreams
And I used to wonder,
Should I procrastinate my dreams for them,
Creating more sleepless nights?

Life is a Bookstore

Sometimes when I know my story
Won't be as shiny as a book,
I will simply cancel my plans
And travel through a book,
Across space, time, and tears.

Reading for pleasure is different
Than reading for requirement;
For I can let my mind wander
With no time constraint
Or pressure to memorize dates.

Reading a plethora of different books,
Has made me laugh and appreciate linguistics.
Developing my own style of words on paper,
I guess that's also why I talk
Like a wordsworth and a gangster.

Heels & Hoodies

Nothing is more cozy,
And makes your cheeks feel as rosy,
Than the warm hug of an oversized hoodie.

But my confidence is at its crest
When I wear long gowns
That hug my every curve and imperfection.

Accentuated by baby pink mary jane pumps,
Bringing my confidence and height 3 inches
taller,
With my Tiffany-blue watch coldly caressing my
warm supple skin.

Though removing all these components one by
one,
And watching my makeup swirl in watercolors
down the drain,
Makes the hug of my oversized hoodie just a bit
warmer.

Emblem of Gems

16

The best gems are the ones on a whim,
Not mass-produced or well-known,
With a meaningful memory tucked within.
With a look so unique,
It's impossible for others to guess a backstory.
These best gems are quirkily invaluable.

Crystals On-Call

A stroll into a crystal shop,
Leads to an involuntary gawk of adoration.
Hundreds of crystals piled on shelves to eternity,
And one special one is yours.

Whether brittle, gold, or artificial stone,
Raw from earth or polished to perfection,
Towers of amethyst or a penny-sized aqua opal,
Just make your cheeks turn a rose quartz pink.

Crystals hailing from Bristol to Boston,
With all sorts of hidden backstories,
Crystals can give you stylish safety,
As seen when the evil eye bracelet breaks.

Christmas Day is Everyday

Nothing conjures more childlike joy,
Than slicing the tape of mailed boxes
Or tearing open an envelope in excitement.
Knowing your package came from vast lands,
You may desire to visit or miss dearly.

The brief moment opening a package,
And sensing the passion in a handwritten note
Through swirly letters and blotches of midnight
ink
And maybe even a doodle or unique signature
Is how personality is felt without words.

I Love You *literally* in Thousands of Ways

Oh, to know multiple languages.
Discovering new festivals, traditions, and
superstitions
Knowing how to say I love you in multiple ways
Mahal Kita, Te Amo, Je t'aime

Understanding the humor that binds cultures,
Connecting you to corners the world,
You may have never set foot upon,
Or that your heart yearns to return to.

Though the purest of conversations
Are between two people unknowing of each
other's native tongues
Trying to converse through theatrical hand
gestures
For smiles are the true universal language.

Scattered & International Love

As the daughter of a Filipina immigrant,
I appreciate dearly the opportunities in America,
As well as the unprecedented hospitality of
Filipinos
Even calling me "Ms. Universe" for my olive
skin,
The perfect combination of dad's milky skin and
mom's tan pigment.

While I can't think of anything more flattering,
I sometimes wonder what it's like to be my
mom,
And spark immediate friendship with Filipinos
abroad
Exchanging phone numbers and stories of home,
Instead of being viewed as "Miss. Americana".

As I see my mom's tears and nostalgia returning
to her homeland,
Laughing and joyfully yelling untranslatable
idioms,
I simply admire her immense homely happiness.
Though sometimes I wish I could understand her
native tongue,

Instead of hearing the translated version after the
climax of laughter disintegrates.

Whether it be mahal kita or I love you,
America will always be my home I know and
love.
But thousands of miles away,
Across thousands of islands,
My heart is scattered vicariously through my
mom's journey.

1am Escapades

The most magical ideas blossom at 1am,
Which is when this poem was written.
For tense nerves of stress in an overthinking
mess
Slowly melt away into the twilight night sky,
But with just enough energy for productive fun.

Whether it be grinding on study nights,
Losing track of reading time,
Or having your eyes glued to that one show,
Everything seems a little more peaceful and
unweighted,
And become unforgettable memories or
once-in-a-century discoveries.

Whether it be living life to the fullest,
Or studying books to the fullest,
1am is the hour all the brightest stars are up.
Which is why this poem is saved as last,
During the best and first hour of the day.